The Ruby Slippers

Helen Burke was born in Doncaster, 1953, and started writing poetry in the 1970s. Since then she has amassed an impressive record of competition victories, including the Manchester International, the Suffolk Poetry Prize, and the Ilkley Literature Performance Poetry Prize (twice).

Her work has been published in *Rialto*, *New Welsh Review*, *Northwords*, *Dreamcatcher*, as well as in numerous pamphlets and anthologies. *The Ruby Slippers* is her first full-length collection.

The Ruby Slippers

HELEN BURKE

To Pat

thank-you guys
ain't enough!!

Love Helen
xx

VALLEY

THE RUBY SLIPPERS

First published in 2011
by Valley Press
www.valleypressuk.com

Printed in England by Imprint Digital,
Upton Pyne, Exeter

The right of Helen Burke to be identified as author
of this work has been asserted in accordance with Section
77 of the Copyright, Designs and Patents Act 1988

ISBN: 978-0-9568904-3-6
IPN: VP0015

A catalogue record for this book
is available from the British Library

www.valleypressuk.com/authors/helenburke

9 8 7 6 5 4 3 2 1

CONTENTS

for Phil

in memory of
Mum, Dad and Bob

Introduction

'Why I Write'

You ask me why I write...

And this is why.

Because I've had arthritis for forty years – you don't get that for murder – and it's my way of making the pain go away. I write because my mum couldn't spell, but knew more about the novels of Thomas Hardy than I do. I write because my dad could tell an Irish story so well – you believed you were in the heart of Dublin itself, just downing a Guinness and starting several arguments, all at the same time. That's why I write – so it is.

I write because if I didn't the sun would stop shining, the moon would stop everything else, the storm at sea would get bored and go home and the whirlwind would cave in on itself and become just a breeze.

I write because two and two don't make four. Because inside every butterfly is a caterpillar trying to get out. Because blue will never be red and tomorrow, when you've almost given up hope – the birds really will sing. And my legs will dance again. That's why I write.

I write because there is a blackbird on the wall outside and there is a soft rain falling on the last rose of summer in the hedge and sometimes it's easy to forget the good times and only see the bad.

I write because somewhere Phil is reaching up to paint a corner of a room, and dancing on the ceiling for me in someone's house. And dreaming of sitting with me by a lake in Italy – and being happy, like they are in films.

I write because if you love someone, you help them climb a mountain. Because at the top of the mountain – there are no more words. Only a never-ending truth and the thing you've been writing about – except the two of you didn't know it. That's why I write.

Poems are like bandages – they slowly unravel as various cuts and grazes set about healing.

Stories are what I tell when I want to be sure I leave my real footprints in the sand at the edge of this ocean I call my life. I write because I'm a clown who fondly imagines that by being crazy I might just stay sane. That's why I write – so it is. To be sure.

By the way – I love you Phil – that's why I write.

Helen Burke
September 2010

THE RUBY SLIPPERS

Quiet Auditorium

Outside the snow is singing –
there is a knock at the door.
I open it, you are there,
eyes dark-rimmed and solemn round.
I know half of you has stood
there before. You speak snatched words
in the weasel-sharp wind. Outside
an animal is bleeding, you say. You
require a room to rest in, just
to catch your breath, to
have a seat by a fire and
perhaps food – be no trouble, no trouble
before moving on again. Your Spartan
mood unsettles me. I close
my splintered eyes to think –
and opening them, look up to see the heavy
door shut fast. So, the problem is solved

but
what was it, what was I about to say, my
hands are cold, blancmange-like, my heart
is a small box,
wired. Inside the room I can
see a young woman sat reading, while,
through the windows, prickly-steamed,
an animal is warming itself
at the fire. A snow coat forms around me.
Outside the snow is taking its seat, ready
for the next act, but,

it must wait for your cue. Hush –
there is a knock at the door,
get up, get up and put this page down
now,
for it is your door.

Whale

We discussed
when and where whales sleep.
(Even if they do.) How heavy
is a whale's dream? Maybe it can
only dream once a century. All the rest
of its wide-lipped, big-jawed,
muscle-turned, blink-free day – it fits in,
before tackling its first wink,
its first breath, and its last.
Who could stop a whale doing that?

Its swimming is a graceful egg, a perfect
bowl of white lilies, the pure sound
of a Ming vase.
It does not swim, but pipes the ocean
through its veins, once a day –
turns it in one almighty somersault,
straight up, straight over.
The globe, an aristocrat of acrobats,
is a safe tennis-ball in its mouth,
spinning effortlessly – taking
its first breath in with its last,
one long slow breath
before the whale can dream again,
before the Earth should chance to cool –
to spin, to stop.

Tigers

I know there is a beginning and an end to most things
I know that when you're in the middle of two people, one
    feels left out
I know that between today and tomorrow this or that will
    happen
I know that when you say you're not worried that is not
    really how you feel –
I know that to be sure of something, even for one minute,
    holds no eternal guarantee
I know that landscapes where I've lived are still the same –
    it's me that changes, isn't constant
I know the sea has no enemies
I know that time will tell
I know that without permission everything is possible
I know religion is no excuse
I know love is a word in need of translation
I know to start caring again is as hard as to stop –
I know today has no roof and yesterday has no mirror
I know that life is probably not a film someone has made
I know that there are people who never dream
I know that to dream of white means death
I know that to dream of tigers, always of tigers, is unlikely
    and not to be wished for, but nonetheless I do –
and I know that tigers should not be held by their tails.

Another Song

Cutting the road
to a solid edge,
first, the boots welling up –
all dust, and the salt lines,
fresh.
The men start singing, the sweat
rolls down their arms –
the elbows become as sore
as a child's rubbed arms.
My dad's cap is pulled well down,
over tired, dustbin-lidded eyes.
Sometimes he makes me think
of a snowman, all black where the white
should go, and huddled spaces
for the mouth, the eyes.

They come up from the ground,
singing the 'Rose of Tralee' and 'Danny Boy',
climbing up out of the earth –
'grave robbers all of us', they joke – and
'it's our funeral.' Shaking their big fists
at the invading dust.
A part of the road goes home with each of them.

Tomorrow it's pay day.
A good rest tonight, then, a woman
bringing tea in mugs and a thin brown envelope.
Numbered.

Soon, it's Monday again,
and the landlord comes.
'Where's the rent?'
'It's all been spent,' we shout,
sending him on his way
with a flea in his black and blue cap.
Me dad's clean new notes
in his soft-lined pocket and us with
another song to learn
before next week.

On Wearing My Uncle Patrick's Hat

I wonder
how many times did my Uncle's hat
glimpse this old lane?
On his way to Aunt Rose's house perhaps –
the one that got bombed?
Or even half way round the city walls
on the Whit-Walk,
sat like a jaunty owl, on his head.
Later, the hat became my fathers' hat.
It sat on his head, like a raven on the wing.
The wearing of hats to him, always
a thing of mystery.
The hat saw both of them
home from two wars.
It heard talk of a boat to America.
It heard of work to be had and street after
street of Irish good luck,
for the taking.
It saw itself Top of the World.
It imagined a brave new beginning.
Now, I wear the hat –
out in the old lane just a stones' throw
from Rose's.
The ruins of the house.
The secrets of the hat.
I analyse the dust of them both.
They fit me, perfectly.

The Aunts

They sit about my house, the aunts –
drink tea, play cards and laugh.
They sit about my house.
I listen to them.

Sarah, tall and wiry, strong of arm,
and Lella, more delicate, lying
on the sofa, to catch again
her breath.

They sit about my house. I hear the aunts,
their easy talk and laughter,
their tales of people long since gone,
their talk of you.
I hear them best when I remember you.

The sound of their words, soft
doves upon the air –
burrs caught up in downy cloth,
their talk of better days
and times to come.

Sitting, watching the coals glow
in my fireplace – as though
the aunts still breathed on them, they glow.
I breathe in and out with them,
willing them to go on – but even the tallest
of the flames dies away and the last
of the warm embers I see is
also stopped for breath.

The Grenz

Trees, hundreds of them,
slim warriors, leaf-bright blades –
between two of them, he saw
the smallest face.
They were on the Grenz, the border.

To this smallest, frightened face
(that looked from behind the border
that was trees) he made a sign.
My father made the sign of the cross,
called out: 'You have found a friend
in the trees.' (He imparts good news slowly,
with a King's air, still does.) 'How many are you?'
He asked – the voice returned to him, 'forty.'

To take the wrong track at the border
is easily done. So, he must take them
the longest route, but the safe one.
Through the thickest of the forest
they flitted, his own collection of butterflies,
to freer soil.

It was dark before they parted, at the midnight.
Crossing over, the last of them,
turned, made his own sign of the cross to
a face between the trees, a young soldier.
Leaving its shape there, in the wind, just
above his head – a benediction on the front
that chance returned to them their souls.
'How many are you?' The wind returns it, 'forty.'

Racing Caterpillars

Inch by inch, they emerge.
(We have a matchbox each.)
The path next to the cabbages is cold, grey.
And there's been rain. Good Yorkshire rain,
in hisses and steams in the yard like fighting cocks.
It talks about trouble at the mine and how money
may always be the other fellow's, and how
Dad's job is on the line, but –
we don't have ears that hear this yet.
We are racing caterpillars down by the Big Cut.
We've skived off school – where will that get us
    anyway?
Books and that.
Timing for each caterpillar is crucial.
But we get interruptions.
For now these are called parents and lessons.
Later they will be called marriage and kids.
But today, racing caterpillars, none of this matters.
We have new sandals on that Mam paid half a week's
    wages for.
Our feet were measured for them like a baby's corpse.
We have sherbet lucky dips lolling from our pockets.
We have used your maths test as the starting-line.

Now we can see them. The runners emerge from the
   stands.
My caterpillar is too laid back.
It was a mistake to call him Ringo.
In defiance you have called yours Paul. But he is too
   cocky.
You are laughing so much that I know you'll be sick.
So I reckon,
I am in with a chance.
Just this once, eh?

Strange Meeting

You always hurried me on past them.
The crazy twins.
We always knew where we would meet them
(by the beck) – hubble bubble, toil and trouble –
and that they would be jabbering in their
crazy talk – with just those two heads
to hold the one thought.

All in white, with weird aprons, heavy boots
and red patchwork bonnets.
You walked on their side in case they lashed out at us.
I remember their eyes were livid blue
like bruised bluebells and that
their skin was white like
no blood flowed in their veins at all.
They had plaits to their waists
with bright red ribbons
that flapped in the icy tinker's wind.
Their voices were shrill – old kettles
hissing over wild flames.
They had one walk between them.
They had one destination and one eye on it.
'It's a shame,' you always said,
when we were safe at home and sitting by
our different fire. And sadness came.

And I remembered how they steered each other
like two wild ponies but
without looking. How they flew
across the beck, so much quicker than us.
Queens of the night-time blue black air.
The heavy boots making no sound.
The singing kettle in their lungs hanging
in the winter dark.

The Dancing Room

That room.
I remember that room, where
the red darkness
gave itself up to green.
It was a square room.
No, it was a round room.
See, how memory trips me up.
To think that I was ever there now.
To think that my legs contained that much light.
Now, they are strange shadowy horses.
I must pick them up to lead them at all,
as round the green field
they and I, go.
They look at me as if they hardly know me.
'Has it come to this?' They ask.
'Can't you see the light that spills from the dancing
    room?
We can still see it. It is you who is blind.'
They are right.
I remember now. How it goes.
You open the door with your heart, and enter.
Right there where green light shifts
from under the door.
Where no shadows enter, save one.

The white light that comes from dancers –
have you never seen it?
I have bottled it in my mind's eye.
Brought it here for you.
This is how it goes.
It is a ripe fig on a green plate.
It is a monkey swinging its long legs from a silver tree.
It is a red gate that melts inside time, at
your touch.
It is the underbelly, the shadow of dawn that walks
    abroad.
It is the need, and the dream, the being and the not-being
all in one.
It is the place that ends all beginnings.

How the light dazzles me.
It is cruel. It is wonderful.
Today, I am a ripe fig on a green plate.
I am cicada breath in the midnight, still.
I am the red fox who meets himself under the green
    moon.
Today, I am come back to the place I long for.
I can edge myself easily under the door.
The floor is the same, here nothing has changed.
The piano stands open – why did I wait?
My feet are cool roses. I remember this room.

My Red Sandals

My steps have no shadows.
My shoes are red.
It is a particular day.
My mother walks ahead of me.
Her steps make my way easy.
This is called holiday.
My feet have no shadows.
Nor are they strangers.
I am a child.
I am running to the beach in my red shoes.
The sand is made of diamonds and people's thoughts.
The clouds are made of ice-cream.
The sea is itself.
My shoes are good in rock-pools.
My shoes are great over rocks.
My shoes are best on sand. This sand.
The sand is diamonds.
It fills my shoes with its thousand lives.

I can see what the sea thinks.
I want these shoes to last forever.
I want this moment to last always.
Not be swept away.

I am not afraid.

My blood is coral reef. My heart
a sudden pearl.
I am here now and I am here always.

I don't want the sea to swallow my red shoes
so I will leave my dears at the water's edge
where the water can talk to them. And now

I am looking back to the shore.
The sky is orange.
The day is lemon sherbet.
The sea is licking it.
I know everything the sea knows.
My shoes are two red boats
and in the deep of deeps alone I'm standing
and clear as clear my mother walks ahead of me.
My riding high, these waves, will last forever.

Nothing is any trouble.
Nothing is any trouble at all.

Inside my shoes, inside my self, diamonds.

The Gift

Today
as if a gladness, a brightness
in the corner of my eye has gone.
As if a part of this timepiece, my heart,
were missing.
As if a face in the corner of my always room
were hidden.
As if a picture we had worked on –
your stitches, small and graceful –
were folded over, were held in another's arms
and for the moment, stored away.

Mother, a perfume steals over me
that is knotted with time.
It is both dark and light and is fretted like the sea.
The sea, the vast sea
so like the colour of your eyes.

Was it yesterday that we examined rings?
Three of them, silent in small blue boxes.
Three thin gold bands –
one with three white diamonds – 'like faces
shining in the night,' you said.

In the small room, I am sitting with you.
I am just sitting with you.
And we spoke of everything, as always and we
admired the rings, in the evening light,
the delicate, special rings.
Later, you close the boxes, one by one, and
as if in a dream, you hand them to me.
My hand over yours, I take them,
the pale room all around us
as if we are drowning, growing paler –
each wave rising higher than the last,
my hand over yours,
you give me treasure, one last time.

Bless This Handbag

At crucial moments of my life
you will find me ironing.
A trick learnt from my mother.
She always smoothed things out,
made peace between warring parties,
Now, the only creases left are around her eyes.

We meet in town, for coffee
and some sort of a cake.
She says she's taking sugar in tea again,
and perhaps I should.
I don't look well. Much too pale.

I manoeuvre the talk onto politics.
The Gulf, the Catholic viewpoint,
the new outlook on water births, legalising pot.
Undeflected, she overrides me with
a brief statement on
meringue and eggs you couldn't get in the war, then
back we go to my own queer pallor.

I wish I'd put more blusher on.
She toys with me like a footballer, playing me back
    and forth.
Or as if we're in a trench and she can constantly order
    me
over the top.
The confrontation is endless.

I wish I could learn this trick from her.
I wish I knew how the war could be won.
I wish I could eat meringue that fast.

I will my cheeks to glow with health as
she leads me across the No-Man's-Land of
combinations and corsetry of
hosiery appliances, and multi size inner soles.
Everything the colour of a rich tea biscuit.

Playfully, she tweaks at a string vest as we pass.
'Call that a changing room? I wouldn't send a dog in
    there.'
Like a russet bomb, her handbag is ticking.
It is bright scarlet, goes with nothing that she wears.

Patiently, she shows me something that doubles as
an omelette scoop and a thing for killing wasps.
'If you're going to wear green for God's sake, do it on a
Wednesday,'
she says,
and leaves it at that.
We narrowly miss a rail of pinnies.

Slowly we make our way to the bus stop.
Even this much walking is too much now.

I promise to eat more, but to smoke
and go out less.
She waits for the bus, handbag clutched stoically.

Inside it I can glimpse
two tins of rice pudding
and a bottle of Lourdes water – in case of emergency.
She climbs onto the bus. Hands me a separate package.
It's the third tin of rice pudding.

Even as the bus rounds the corner
I can still see the handbag, gathered to her,
its words of wisdom
like a million sun's rays, glinting, fabulous.
Eradicating all conflict, going over the top.

Sea-Largo

Tonight, I am the sea
cool and calm,
breaking light into sound
and birds into shadow-lanterns.

Tonight, I am the sea.
I am the music of flutes
beguiling the white-lipped spray.
I am this limbo, wild music for you.
Do you hear me calling, calling
against the rocks?

Tonight, I am the sea.
I am the wild and winding wind that
lives deep there.
I am all the creatures that live by the sea alone.

See where I make my bed in the snakes of sand.
See where the foam coils my hair, where my eyes
lap at the edge of shells.
I make the sound the sea makes at night,
beneath the waves I reach for the pulse of stars,
the echo of their song is silence.
Tonight, I am the sea.

Avoiding Stories

Today I am avoiding stories, but everywhere I go things
    happen.
For instance, there is a new man come to clean the
    windows.
He says that my soul is in urgent need of a clean and that
    he –
as an emissary from God's honeycombed lair – can do it.
When I open the door to pay him, he is wearing only a
    bowler hat.
Nothing else.
I do not think he is from God, but just then I am called
    away to the phone.
It is you, to say you are being rushed to casualty as you
    have choked
on a piece of shoe leather which you mistook for beef and
    placed in a sandwich.
It was the piece I had put in the fridge to repair the lucky
    wind-chime someone
bought us, which fell on my foot mangling the top
    phalanx of my big toe.
I call a taxi to the hospital which, when it comes, is being
    driven
by the ex-monk I normally try to avoid. He has taken up
    taxi-ing as it
involves less shenanigans and fewer nuns.
(You can see how my avoidance has failed me, I think.)
We discuss how you can get cheap roof racks at Leeds-
    Bradford airport and how
in fact shoe leather can look like beef in a certain light.

When I get to casualty the receptionist makes me wait as
    long as she can as she
blames me for the fact that she can't retire for eight more
    years as her husband,
who was once in my job club, is still the lazy idle git he
    always was.
I am sent to the wrong cubicle where a vagrant is being
    treated for trapped wind.
Finally, I find YOU. You are now in the recovery
    position despite the fact
you have swallowed the best part of half a sandal.
WE EMBRACE.
A doctor comes in who, taking against my Irish surname,
    asks me if
it is normal Irish practice to leave shoe leather where
    innocent painter-and-decorators
might be tempted to eat it.
I explain I am not Irish, it's just the surname, but she will
    have none of it.
I think she would like a sample of my blood. All of it.
Eventually we manage to leave after a cup of tea from a
    trolley being driven by a man
called Bert who I remember from a watercolour class, as
    Barbara-Who-Likes-Shoes.
(I am reluctant to call another taxi, for fear of monks, so
    we decide to walk home.)
When we get there a group of about twenty gypsies have
    tethered two horses to our front gate
and are racing the third one chariot style down the street.

We sit on our wall and share an apple with the horses.

Sandra is a Child of Peace and Love

Sandra is five foot two.
Sandra is fierce, like Boadicea.
We are on our way to Knebworth
in an old jalopy,
my red hat is floppy and
I've got sandals on
and we've got joss sticks in the van.
Joni Mitchell is playing in the park
and we've borrowed Keith's van and we're off to
Knebworth for a lark.

Sandra works at Woolies –
plastic roses, care of Daz, decorate her hair.
If you can remember Sandra in the sixties
you probably weren't there.
Me – I'm a rebel in my leopard-skin pill-box hat
and Sandra – she's a child of peace and love.

I've been selling Oz magazine in the High Street again,
I'm a student, I'm a rebel, when they call at my door –
me mam's packed me sandwiches, I said I'll be home by
    four –
I've got a dahlia in my hair –
if you can remember me and Sandra –
you just *so* were not there –
me I'm a rebel, quintessential psychedelic,
and Sandra, she's a child of peace and love.

It's 1994, when I meet Sandra again –
she says: 'What you doing now pet?
Do you fancy a cup of tea,
we can nip down to Greggs, I've got the 40p.
Barry? The one with the headband –
he's living in Oz now –
I wish I'd never met him, what a flaming square –
as far as happiness goes, he was definitely not there –
do you remember I was a child of peace and love?'

She says all the bairns have gone
and she's divorced twice now –
she's doing a course in self development – worra laugh –
about bloody time eh?
There are lines around her eyes –
which is no surprise to me, no not at all –
When we pass the flower seller in the Big Market,
I can almost smell that perfume of when we didn't have a
    care –
She says: 'Do you remember?'
I say – of course not – we were there.
I'll always be a rebel. And you are still a child of peace
    and love.

Why I Fancy Him

It's something to do with the way
his shoulders grip life
as he walks down the road to the match.
Like a warrior into battle.
Something to do with the scent of his dreams
on the pillow next to mine.
Something about the way he can't choose
holiday shorts without me. Something about the way he
    stands
while poaching us both an egg and
reading the match results.
Something about the fact that the answer phone buttons
    baffle him.
Something about the way he still manages a smile
as he picks up the forty-fifth shell from the beach,
that JUST might be the one.
Something about his look over the top of the newspaper
when I mention (again) this amazingly cheap trip
to Portuguese monasteries or how you can track down the
Lost Orchid of the Incas and stay with a genuine relative
of Montezuma – if you book early enough.
Something about his dazzling display of monkey walks
that gets us thrown out of an art gallery.
Something about the way he ties up flowers in the garden
trying to make the process both invisible and painless.
Something about the way he gets entangled in his own
    cagoule.
Something about the way he balances casually on top of a
    forty-foot ladder,

and shouts down he'll have a ninety-nine in his cornet,
but no raspberry sauce.
Something about the way he falls asleep reciting a love-
    poem
and cradling a half-eaten banana.
Just, something.

Children's Games

And it's always just like that.
You have to swallow a piece of gum or a part of a clock
and not be seen to be sick or bothered –
or wallop a wild cat with a dead dog's leg and if it
    scratches you
and you get rabies you have to cross yourself six times
behind the priest's back and then you'll live forever.
    Maybe.
And then you have to
nick half a coconut from the fair
AND spit on the shadow of the man who
does the waltzers whose wife has a beard and sits in the
    tent
telling fortunes where if you hear what she's said, even
    one word –
you'll grow an extra foot, or an extra arm – or both –
and you'll be like old Crutchy Miller that lost his with the
    gangrene.
And it's always just like that.

And then you have to
touch the mad nun's skirt and run quick as hell
past Jimmy the Tramp who used to be a darts player
until the slings and arrows of the world got to him –
just like mam says they got to dad.
And it's always, always, just like that.
Then.
You have to run away from home and live rough in
a tent on the big skip where people say

there once was a murder, and then you have to breeze
    back
in at home and ask: 'so what's for tea?' – and not cry if
they didn't even notice you was gone.
Then.
You have to walk real calm and lay your head down
like a Sunday offering on the railway-lines –
and leave it there, and leave it there, and leave it there –
    until
someone with ginger hair and muddy trousers goes past
(and it's got to be BOTH, just one doesn't count)
and they shout: 'Hey Mad Nellie One Eye – get yourself
    home
your tea's on't table fresh from't chippie. And – is it true
    they've taken back your telly?'

And then you've got to run all't way home and unless –
    and only IF –
your mam's dead, not tell anyone that you've locked your
    cousin
in her dad's allotment shed –
BUT – if your mam's dead –
you can let on after tea.
And it's always, always, just like that.

And IF they ask,
and even if you're not scared like Jimmy Cagney wasn't in
   that film
where his friend the priest begs him and all –
and he dies pretending to squirm and be a rat –
don't let on about none of it.
Except if absolutely EVERYONE in the world is dead.

And then you can only own up to the coconut.

The Ruby Slippers

You come in to the shop with me and
we take my new false leg off and
look around for an assistant but
they all seem to be very busy breathing and
polishing the shoes in the window.
Which is strange because they don't look the polishing
    type.
I have seen the pair I want.
They are red and exotic of course and
I would like to point to them but
a small elderly man comes out from the back-room
(where I think he has been in storage since 1940)
makes eye-contact with you and asks you what you
    would like.

You say you would like to be treated like a normal
    human being.
All the assistants stop polishing now, to listen.
Which is strange because they don't look the listening
    type.
The man says he fought in a war for people like us
and where has it got him?
Then he accidentally knocks my wheelchair and has to
    make eye-contact
with me which is painful to him. Just like the war was.
Then, he wheels me to where they keep
the selection of trainers that nobody buys, and walks off
    back to 1940.

We were happy before we came in.
We had bought chocolates and Parma ham and
we were oh so happy.
Now, you are frothing at the mouth and I have fixed
that smile on my face
like Harry Corbett, when he used to say –
'Bye bye, everybody, bye bye.'
when Sooty had done something wrong and he was
covered in flour and water.

Then, as if by magic – the ruby shoes get up and walk
out of the window
and climb up onto my knee and apologise.

And all the assistants suddenly want to open doors for
us and bow and scrape and help us get the Hell out.
Which is strange because they don't look the opening
doors type.
So, we leave, with those ruby slippers clinging on to us
for dear life and
I want to say: 'Don't you know – I'm fighting in a war
for people like you.'

But, I don't. And Kansas? It just gets further and
further away.

Home Town

This is his home town only because
he doesn't know how to leave.
The way out involves time-tables.
He has trouble with them.
This is his home town.
This is where he cleans his teeth.
Like a bruise, he is not sure how he got here.
Just that he is here.
He offers strangers crisps.

He stands at train-stations
looking at maps.
Eyes as big as gob-stoppers.
'Skegness, it's so bracing,' the poster says.
He wonders where it is.
Once he went to Leeds but
he kept his eyes shut and so
the memory is blurred.
He has come to call for Peter.
Peter is his mentor, rides ladies' bikes
and thinks he's from the moon.

We ask him where he's from, he says
a hospital in Middlesbrough.
His mother had him there because of Aunty Sadie
and her breeding dogs like.
He's never known his dad.
It seemed the best for all concerned.
Though sometimes on his birthday
he wonders if he's dead.

This is his home town, his I'm-in-chains-
grown-cold town.
He used to be a window cleaner, but
didn't like heights.
He could only do the bottom ones and people
can be funny. Now
he works at the bookies but has never seen a horse.
He stands and watches trains.
Watches people boarding them
and offers strangers crisps.

The Green Field

I dreamed I was a horse
and the green field all around me
kissed my feet.
In my eyes two doves smiled
and the sun and moon were mine
in equal measure.
The day was music within my bones.
The night was music within my blood
and I was blessed.

And blessed
I ran within that green field, where,
in its sweetest, farthest corner I saw
lay buried, a silver-box – so small,
yet within the box,
lay the root, the tree,
the waiting forest of my dreams.

And from this, I ran.
And ran, and ran, far far from it, until –
at last, I saw it no more –
and was sad.
For years I ran and ran and ran – until –
the moon it was that stopped me. Under her light,
I looked down and saw that
within my own body lay that green field,
within my own heart lay that silver box.
Still and silent – in the moon's light.

Waiting.

Wing

The sea is a single blue banana
pouring into an envelope of
complete light.
There are no patches of mist in this sky,
no question of silver in this sea.
How easy it all makes itself here.

Further along the road today, we came
to a small hedge, on it lay
on oyster-grey, smooth, slicked back
abandoned gull's wing.
The wing that could be my own. In fact,

you laugh and say you are sure it is
and now I look closer – I recognise it
and remember the loss.
I replace it carefully, at my outer and thinnest
edge, under my ragged sword wing, my battle arm.

There is not enough room for it, it seems to me,
but, you take it from me and show me where it fits,
(how easy you make it look) saying –
'Come, let us share the wing. For it seems to me,
we are in the same sky.'

Owls

Tonight,
the moon is a river.
A silver shadow whose face we admire.
The moon turns the river's pages
like a book.
Softly, the pages turn, one by one.
In the river ourselves, our faces, turning.
Here, where the edges of trees frisk our shadows
and trace the night shapes of houses –
we are watching for owls.
I am convinced they are near.

It is only that the dark trees are hiding them.
It is only that the old boats are hiding them.
The owls fly inside my own eyes – in and in,
flying lower and lower. My thoughts become feathers.
My dreams have no edges. Flight swallows me.
I am owl and moon and river and night.
The stars watch over me – the pulse of the water
greets me, keens for me
that I must watch here, so late. It is the hour for owls.
I hear the slow beating of their coming.
A train passes, holds the moon in each of its windows.
Myself, I am held by the promise of owls.
My throat holds a shadow, it grows and grows
and from it
flies the first of them.

At the Foreigners' Club

At first, at the Foreigners' Club
we wear our English-ness with pride.
It is expected of us.
We say: 'Bring us your finest marmalade –
but not your marmite, for we have brought our own
in small tartan shoppers bought in Epping.'
We ask how the eggs are fried and if
the man who batters the fish
comes from a real family of batterers. (If not, we send
    it back.)

In the huge Venetian mirrors, the waiters
move serenely like tall ships
moving in and out of difficult harbours.
They all sing – though one whistles – 'Figgy Pudding.'

There is a strange English-ness about him.
The other waiters hoot and toot and call out:
'Mamma Mia – we are having you replaced Figgy
    Pudding.
There is always tomorrow to be English –
be English when you are dead.
Right now we are bringing you Neapolitan ice-cream
made by our own grandmothers.'

We hitch up our baggy shorts and leave the bar inside
(with its pots of tea and trifle) empty.
We drift outside to a boulevard of pistachio and a peach
    sunrise.
We lie on the grass like emperors – our
skin speckled with icing sugar, rose petals and violets.
    (What devils we are.)

For a little while we watch the vanilla sunset.
For a little while, we are Italian.

On the 14th Deck of the Cruise Ship Aurora

No-one wears beige on the fourteenth deck.
No-one wears sailor suits and plays deck quoits.
No-one invites us to a chocoholics buffet or
asks thirty Indian chefs to limbo-dance
through a gateaux of mousse-lined Viking ships.
There is a strange light from this Captain's eyes.
This floor is made of Cape daises and kept promises.
The portholes glisten with honeysuckle and ragged robin.
The Captain wears nothing and he advises we do the same.
Things are different here.
Our bodies become young again and softly entwined in
    each other.
The flowers become entwined in our bodies, until
between flesh and flowers there is no difference.
Here, the moon keeps time in its small hand and the sun
    plays a mandolin.
It is a medley of voices we had thought lost forever.
There is a river we may bathe in and become free again.
Our hearts are happy as drooping fuchsias that nod in time
to the road that leads to the sea.
Our foxglove fingers and forget-me-not souls will not be
    parted.
We break and bend in the wind from the ocean as if we
    were one person.
Our old skin uncurls from the body like an onion-ring
and our new self uncurls and touches the stars.
On the fourteenth deck, all is known – and no-one is a
    stranger.
Even those who never met, remember where it was.

The Captain has a bugle in the shape of a moose with huge
    crystal antlers.
This moose calls down the sky and calls up the sea
and where the two meet – a young deer and a lion walk.
The Captain is measuring the clouds and the deer and the
    lion walk together freely.
All problems disappear here.
There is no yesterday or tomorrow on the fourteenth deck,
there is only NOW –
lovely, glorious, carefree hope-filled NOW.

Push the button in the lift, my love, and take me there.

The Rehabilitation Hobbies Room

This is recuperation then, this is rehabilitation.
Here by learning how to re-tie my own anxiety into bows
I will be made whole again.
From all the hobbies on the hobby table
I shall choose sand. Sand and ribbon-reading.
By my ribbons they will know me.
I send back the mirrors made from pasta twirls.
I send back the soft toy dogs made from
cotton wool and silly tape.
The gnomes and plaster cast of Jesus (the champagne
corks still wobbling) I eschew.
These are the glories of the hobby room
where we must come before they sign us out, we
    damaged moths.

I must sketch my own silhouette in beer can tops and
draw my own eyes with sea-foam and silicone.
I must re-join my bones with cement and sloe-gin.
I must position my mended shadow on the wall of
    reason.
I must play football with my own spleen,
badminton with my own kidney.
I must leave a sample of my own cheerfulness in the cup
    provided.
I must fashion a prophecy from eggshells and straw.
My hobby is leaving – this is my choice.
I will not choose another.
My lilac wings are beating a pattern in the clear space
    above my head.

Stay in Touch

'You will, won't you – you WILL stay in touch,' she said.
'Of course,' we said – well,
that's to say, we tried.
Wrote letters, sent photos, even once a present.
(What a couple of fools.)
But it seemed life was busier for her than us.
So we never heard squat.
Then ten years later, she saw us in the town, and wept.
'I would have stayed in touch, but, it's just not my forte –
things got on top of me,
the years and jobs and men.
But, NOW, the kids have gone
(moved to the moon to be nearer their dad).
Now I've nothing else doing and I'm miserable as sin
and I'm throwing a breakdown party this very Saturday,
now my life no longer fits or suits me.
You both MUST come. I simply won't take no for an
    answer.

Yes – this time – I really WILL stay in touch.'

Drawing Dogs

I have taken to drawing dogs.
They have begun to seem more like people than people.
I feel more certain that they will
inherit the Earth.
I feel safer when a dog snarls
than when a person smiles.
I can see them deciding not to think of all the answers
before they've eaten their dinner.
I can see they're not bothered if the post is late or if
they miss the bus to Fulham Broadway.
Their faces do not pose when you look at them
(and then try to pretend that they've just seen you).
If they're happy, they're happy – and sad if they're sad.
If they got begging letters – they would answer all of them.
In their heads, all of them are riding motorbikes across
    France
without a care in the world.
And most brilliantly of all – they do not write poetry.
I like dogs.

The Shape of Hands

Mother,
your bright shadow with me all the day.
Like a distant butterfly. All the day.
Hidden by the sun.

Unable to catch sight of your flight,
I look at the space you have left.
I am just too slow, too intent and though
I look and look,
I miss where you fly, how your wings are unclaimed
by the heaviness of day.
Above me, all around me, your shadow wings a new song.

On the wall, the shadow of my own hand
as night falls.
I look and see it is
the exact shape of yours,
even the way it holds the light against
the outstretched glove of darkness. Incredible how
the cupped shape is the same.

Darkness falls, and though I cannot see the lines
that court this shadow palm, borrowed from you –
I know your flight still follows me.
Together we will see the journey out
trace our shapes against a different sky, but for now
we have spent the day together, after all.

Tomorrow

Tomorrow, there will be enough
of food, and warmth and love, and hope.

Tomorrow, the birds WILL sing.

Tomorrow, fear and hate will be outlawed
and dreams, good dreams, will have a place
in everybody's lives.

Tomorrow, the birds WILL sing.

Tomorrow, there will be no more calls to arms,
to war.
No more pitting soul against soul
until even the bravest dies a little inside.

Tomorrow, the birds WILL sing.

Tomorrow, you will see there is
a reason to go on,
a light that shines,
a field that beckons –
in truth, there will be all you ever hoped for.
You will walk in peace
in the green field, under the sun
that warms, that mends.

Until then, take heart, friend
and be glad you live.
Touch each life you meet
with your own truth
and with this just and certain hope –

Tomorrow, the birds WILL sing.
For each, for everyone.

The Road Out of Town

When will I take you, I ask –
the road out?
Will it be tomorrow? Will it?

Oh, let it be tomorrow –
sweet as a peach that road
and you, juicy with laughter.
Rich that road, as rich as rich
with peacock beginnings
and myself with the shackles and the blindfold gone
and this other road – forgotten.
At first we will be dizzy with the joy of it
but that won't matter – no –
just the feel of the road under our feet
shaking the dust of ages,
the cruel hands of time from ourselves.
Just the being Gone will be enough.

No barriers. No signposts.
Just the sun shining on new black tar.
The smell of it under our feet.
And my little famine bones, mending again.
With each bold step as further out of town
I with my singing heart and my whistling soul am led.

And you will look around – oh yes
and only know that I am gone.
You will see the space I have left and say:
'Why yes – there was somewhere else she had to be,
a path she always had to tread'

and you will hear me singing still
as all sing when first they take that single step
on the Road out of Town.

NOTES

on

THE RUBY SLIPPERS

Quiet Auditorium (p. 13) – This was one of the first poems I ever had published. It won a prize and a place in an anthology of poetry judged by the poet Vernon Scannell, launched at Ilkley Literature Festival. It was one of the first poems I wrote after returning to live in Yorkshire from Birmingham. I moved to a house that dated from the 1600s, a house that seemed to have many 'ghosts'. I would almost say they wrote the poem.

Whale (p. 15) – This poem came out of a conversation with my dad about what a whale's dream must be like. It made me wonder so much, after he had gone home (I think we had been to the pub) I wrote the poem. It went on to win the York Poetry Competition judged by Ian McMillan.

Tigers (p. 17) – This poem was written at a writing workshop run by a very young Simon Armitage! I remember he particularly liked the line: 'without permission, everything is possible.' It was one of those poems that seem to come out of nowhere – I have read it as a finale piece to many readings over the years. It has become a bit of a credo.

Another Song (p. 18) – This was another poem inspired by my dad – the background was when he used to be a labourer, building roads and laying gas pipes in and around York. They were an interesting bunch of men, mainly Irish. I have also written a short story about them, 'The Holy Grail'. 'Danny Boy' mentioned in the poem was my dad's favourite song, and it was sung at his funeral. The poem was published in a Hull anthology of poetry, and was also read at Hull Literary Festival, accompanied by the musician Simon Davey playing 'Danny Boy'.

On Wearing My Uncle Patrick's Hat (p. 20) – This was a poem written about my Uncle Pa, who died when I was eight. He was a very quick-witted man, who served in the Boer War, and was usually a winner in the Whit Walks in the city. I wrote the poem while wearing his trilby hat bought at the local co-op in the 1930s. The poem has now been translated into Romanian – also read on Romanian (BBC) radio, and featured in an Anglo-Romanian anthology and CD.

The Aunts (p. 22) – This poem is about the two Irish aunts who brought my dad up after his parents died, Lella and Sarah. Because where I live isn't far from their house, I often feel there is a certain continuity to life and their stories. This poem won the Suffolk Poetry Prize, judged by Anthony Thwaite (originally from Yorkshire!) It was also published in *Rialto*.

The Grenz (p. 23) – This was a poem about a real incident that happened to my dad when he was serving in the Second World War. Under cover of darkness he smuggled some refugees to safety. The poem won the Manchester International Poetry Prize in 1996 and was read at the prize giving there. This was the first poem I ever read in public, at Nellie's Bar in Beverley.

Racing Caterpillars (p. 24) – This poem is published for the first time here. It was written as a fun piece about the caterpillars in matchboxes that my cousin Catherine and I used to race at my Aunty Mary's house. I never had a pet – these were the nearest I ever got to one!

Strange Meeting (p. 26) – This is about two identical twins who lived near me as a kid. My mum and I would often pass them and – because they dressed in very old fashioned clothing – to me as a child, it was a little scary. The poem was published by York St. John's University in their student magazine while I was studying a Literature MA there.

The Dancing Room (p. 28) – Before I got arthritis, I did ballet dancing for many years in York. It was my big passion in life – I did several stage shows and hoped to make dancing my career. I try to dance with words now – and wanted to capture my lost world in this poem. At time of writing, 'Dancing Room' has just been commended in the William Soutar House Competition, and will be available at the House there in an anthology of the winning poems.

My Red Sandals (p. 30) – This poem has not been published previously, but it has been done as a collagraph print by myself. I didn't have Ruby Slippers as a child – but I did have an amazing pair of red sandals – *Start Rite!* – which I loved. In the poem they represent innocence, timelessness – childhood itself, almost.

The Gift (p. 32) – This poem was the 'title track' of the CD I brought out in 2000. It is the one poem on the CD I struggled to read because it is about my mum, who was an incredibly strong character. The boxes referred to in the poem contained her wedding ring and her engagement ring. She gave them to me when she knew she was quite ill; they are the only gold I have. I still wear them.

Bless This Handbag (p. 34) – This poem is published for the first time here. It is about my mother's handbag, which went everywhere with her. It was a kind of talisman and a standing joke between us that I never liked it, because it didn't go with anything. It is quite true that she often had rice pudding or chicken soup in it, just in case of an emergency.

Sea-Largo (p. 37) – This poem was published in *Dreamcatcher* magazine. The sea was very important to my mum – she was only really happy by the sea. I wanted to capture that feeling of complete joy in this poem.

Avoiding Stories (p. 38) – Written much later than the preceding poems, while living back in the city and trying to do lots of different courses and workshops – trying things on for size, if you will. A bit chaotic, my life, at this time.

Sandra is a Child of Peace and Love (p. 41) – This poem was published in an anthology of material from a stage show I did for about two years. The show was called 'Subterranean Homesick Yorkshire Blues' and toured to several festivals and theatres. 'Sandra' in the poem was a girl I knew in the sixties/early seventies when I was a student in Newcastle. The Knebworth concerts were a pilgrimage for us – they were very happy days.

Why I Fancy Him (p. 43) – This poem has not been published before. It is about my partner, and I hope is self-explanatory!

Children's Games (p. 45) – This poem won the 'Yorkshire Prize' within the Yorkshire Poetry Competition. It is an unusual poem in that it has a repeat rhythm – and almost a kind of lyric feel to it. All the games mentioned in the poem, I played as a kid – these were an only child's games, an Anglo-Irish child's games – Catholic, wild and obsessive.

The Ruby Slippers (p. 48) – This poem has just been waiting for this book. It is a true story of shoe-shopping in a wheelchair – a task I do not recommend to you, on any level. Those Ruby Slippers are the only ones for me, and – like Cinderella's glass one – they seem to fit me perfectly. Published here for the first time.

Home Town (p. 50) – This poem won the Devon Dorset Poetry Prize. It is about a real person that my partner knew at the time. I hope it is quite poignant about their life – that struggle to leave somewhere, but to be tied to a place with nowhere else to really go.

Green Field (p. 52) – Published in *Dreamcatcher* magazine. 'The Green Field' is also now a children's story I am writing; it has come to symbolise the fruition of everything I have tried to aim for in life. I suppose it is an idyllic place – an Ithaca I hope to reach one day. Here's hoping.

Wing (p. 53) – This poem was published in the pamphlet *Leros: An Island of Dreams*. I went to Greece for three weeks as part of a walking tour to look for a very rare orchid. *Wing* was written while on the island of Leros – as were one or two of the other Greek poems. Another of these was published in *Psychopoetica*, together with some photos of the island.

Owls (p. 55) – Originally a performance piece at the Suffolk Poets 'Schubertiad' in 2010. This was a Viennese-inspired evening and the poem was followed by wonderful piano music by Holger Aston.

At the Foreigners' Club (p. 56) – Previously unpublished. I have visited Sorrento several times now, and would say Italy is my favourite country – the Foreigners' Club is an extraordinary place with a view across Sorrento Bay that is incredible. I hope the poem captures something of the joy and exuberance of the Italian people.

On the 14th Deck of the Cruise Ship Aurora (p. 58) – This poem was written while travelling to the Baltic on a cruise ship. There is no fourteenth deck on the ship concerned – but this was my imagining of what might be up there. This poem has often been performed at readings, but has never been published before.

The Rehabilitation Hobbies Room (p. 60) – Won second prize in the Ver Poets Open Competition 2010. It was inspired by myself, on the road to recovery after numerous leg operations. It was published in the competition anthology.

Stay in Touch (p. 61) – This poem is part of a small origami booklet printed and distributed in Rhode Island. These booklets are distributed to many different venues around the Island by the Origami Poets – Jan Keough and Lynne Gobeille, whose inspirational brainchild this whole project is. This poem is in my first booklet with them.

Drawing Dogs (p. 62) – This poem is the lead poem of my third booklet with the Origami Poets.

The Shape of Hands (p. 63) – This poem about my mother was published in *Rialto*. It is that strange sense of seeing a person who is no longer here, through your own image. Hands, I feel, are a very evocative image.

Tomorrow (p. 64) – This poem, like the much earlier one 'Tigers', has become a major poem for me – it makes a statement of how I hope life could one day be. That sense of waiting for tomorrow is crucial to me as I have had arthritis now for forty years. So, tomorrow is for me, when that will end.

The Road Out of Town (p. 66) – A poem written especially for this book, to close and bring an end to all these landmark steps as I've travelled my own 'Yellow Brick Road.' Maybe, when I get to the Emerald City, I will find out what it has all been about. It has been a hurricane – and Kansas is still a very long way off – but like Ithaca, what the journey and the poems have given me has, I believe, been worth it.

Helen Burke
16th March 2011
(at 11:11!)